Recreational Vehicles on Fire

POEMS BY

Jane Ormerod

THREE ROOMS PRESS
New York

Recreational Vehicles on Fire

ACKNOWLEDGEMENTS
Appreciation to the following publications, in which some of these poems have appeared: Alibi (BigCityLit); Mindapologies (Night Train)

Design: Kat Georges Design, New York (katgeorges.com)

First Edition

Printed in the United States of America

ISBN: 978-0-9840700-1-5

Printed in the United States of America

Text set in Sabon LT Std Roman 10/14

Published by
Three Rooms Press, New York

www.threeroomspress.blogspot.com
www.myspace.com/threeroomspressms
threeroomspress@mac.com

CONTENTS

for Pete

HURRICANE

Not old enough
Just tall enough
I am the original full stopper of
all manner and matter of facts

breathe . . .
breathe . . .

I see fur-lined hats, carpets, ointment, pig squeals, apothecaries
A new town rising then sinking inside this fairground heat
I see a wharf, rows of devil's rope, wild hickory abundant

but never . . .

Just tall enough
I see my great great and great grand family
Hinter, ton, minster, good mother east upon the water
Wheelwrights, blacksmiths, whitesmiths, railway
porters and sleepers, powderers, bed sitters
and publicans wiping hands and tankards

This is the day they lost the talking horse
This is the day they lost the talking horse
This is the day they lost the talking horse

Knock!
He goes outside to masturbate
Knock!
Grazing rights, hunting rights

A roe deer doe in a rodeo
A roe deer doe on the radio
A roe deer doe in a rodeo
A roe deer doe on the radio

English cowboy thoughts below the silver buckle
I prefer the fifth way
Salt warped windmills ever turning
Raindrop faces, elegant fire life
A boy muttering redemption
in full ignorance of rhyme

There are more versions of distance
than should ever be allowed
And tradition?
How do you begin to ever count the ways?

breathe . . . nearly . . .

Using philosophy like leftover turkey
(lost a tenner, found a fiver)
I live within my own forearms
My severed head still grips a pipe
Ah, it was the bicycle not the fish
that made the woman who she was before
the crash and whistle
and the thunder of her legs

Satisfactory wood thrushes
Speckled mothers spitting blessings
Caped sisters, prayers of parts three to five
Wooden ships pushed into glass harmonicas

Rumors that fit the barstool rules today
if not tomorrow

breathe . . .

The loss and profit of the men
dressed in their midnight mid-thigh gowns
The memories of earthworms
Chocolate dripping over a boy child's rattle
The noon fog and summer snow and glory years

Look over there!
See the quintessential twentieth century party
A man with bombshell eyes
Musicians, platters and pitchers, knickerbocker glories
Neapolitan ices and pinch-cheeked ladies
with hearts of Vesuvius

How does the pre and the post and the nerve
and never of a brother form the way you become?

I cannot find him
Lost between the faded blue
I cannot find him
Delicate and estuarial and almost holy

breathe . . .

This is the day they lost the talking horse
This is the day they lost the talking horse
This is the day I believe my brother, Dennis, died

HAPPY
new
YEAR

Pilferers. Philanderers
A merriment dance with those (mad from necessity)
folk-hearted men and their ringletted
ring-footed loves

You don't get it
Just count the simple cost of simple icing
on the simpleton's hurrah cake
Energy loss, the implication of ticks
Tape to rewind a mouth

Halt! Right there!

This is your home in the sun
The place where you toss your teeth on the bed
after unclenching them for mummy

Yummm
(Sell it, buy back with discount, seal it with a piss)

You would prefer life if I vanished all together
Flooring the crowd with your impersonations
of *haven't a clue*
Remembering too late the advice of being nice
to those standing any-old-hows on the ladder
on the ledge, on the curb
To know when to duck, when to comb, and
when to learn basketry

Relegated to penning jingles for off-the-wall funerals
You callous bitch

Heat
Moisture
Meringue for dessert
What else do you require?
More wine? A priest for your sins?
A damehood? A manger? A pilot?
More eggs to crack pretending they are oysters?
A stalking hat? A plot to finish
like *pfff pfff pffffff* away?
A face like a memory of someone once who mattered?

Time bucks too, we used to laugh
Tom Waits for no man

Asses, arses, triple-titted women
with wounds that matter
and necks that easily support a noose

Doors shrinking to indents
Cherries before more snow
My children kill
My children kill
They linger by stairwells
Pixilated, prized apart, re-proportioned
Unable to worthy any trust
Eardrums, concrete, plastic, plaster, slugs of oil
Scented missiles, carpet bags, insecticide
Pigs with hearts of burgers

Read this—
It's all so important
The way most people are normal and you
are some kind of superstarred forecast
with several discernable variables

SMALL FERRY

TO THE FUTURE

lilt   lilt   press pass press

meeting round the corner like the would-be-lovers
they will almost never be

crumple
stilt
skin   heaven heaving brown

the girl with the weight and the cost of a woman

hole   tick   wail   tick holler coat

the merry deal of thunder

meeting round a simple corner
like the blinded whisper
c
h
a
o
s

splayed death horse umbrella outside the
regency hotel
her bottom lip against his top
meager clouds straggling bonanza sky
fingers pushing into teeth
face clean as the easily mesmerized
dark as early approval   bonanza!
coinage euthanasia mounting up in jars
plastic flags   junk coffee   slides
golf miniatures   pennies spending fountains

clink!

last night she scribbled through this darkness
black hint of sleeping beak and feather
deluxe deluxe
tuxedo loosened sky   unicycles made for two
his mind rain trickling on the wrong
side of a window   the rind inside the stone
moon beneath the blame or picture

press

vanilla swirl of ice-cream hair
perambulatory pearls
nearby the old ones teeter   dreaming shipwrecked
homes   silhouettes from a shuffle
a beach floating floating
towards the gilt-head of horizon
what a scorcher! what a stunner! what a tonic!

lilt

dropping deeper into springtime splendor
incense innocence incense innocence in case
out out out then in and further in
smoke hill blue line distance
one sheep encircled by thirty-five shepherds

charcoal knock-kneed foal   tractor parts
and brakes   his disbelief
her dress shorter than the first gasp of a yawn
she is synchronizing efficient air solutions

pass

another dusktime
pinecones tumbling onto pensioners
the two not-so lovers enthusing agreeing
interrupting interpreting
tossing words back and forth like pebbles
watching them grow to rocks or weary into sand

little miss head in the clouds little miss skippy
a flibbertigibbet

jump jump jump skip
be at the end of the seen it all before . . .

mummy is a caterpillar
tildy's whoops! a daisy
daddy told me eat more greens
and boo boo's eyes went crazy

my back's a seat, my front a bench
my face is in, my head is out
my ear is thick, my piece not done
I'm cindy rella bella trout

I'm hooping cock, I'm bella trout
as fox cries fowl and pigs sound shrill
I'm barking sad, a howling tooth
out of kilt but dressed to spill

HELLO, I'M JOHNNY CASH

Hello, I'm Johnny Cash
Recreational vehicles on fire

Hello, I'm Johnny Cash
Recreational vehicles on fire

Hello, I'm Johnny Cash
Recreational vehicles on fire
On fire, on fire, on fire

We support local clean renewable energy by
recycling each and every one of
our recreational crimes
Recreational vehicles on fire
Recreational vehicles on fire

Hello, I'm Johnny Cash
Hello, I'm Johnny Cash
Hello, I'm Johnny Cash
Hello, I'm Johnny Cash

The Big Rig Recreational Gentlemen's Club
is for truckers only
It's the way that it is
It's the way that it is
It's the way that it always is is
The ribs of horizon
De-wilderment, death in separate vehicles
Eyes coloring then fall

Recreational vehicles on fire
Recreational vehicle on fire
Hello, I'm Johnny Cash
Hello, I'm Johnny Cash

At the end of the dream . . . whack . . . September
At the end of the misery stroke love
Alma, Spinach Capital of the World
Alone like elastic, spittoons
Like birds swifting limes
Remember! Remember!
It's easy! The muscles, the lifetimes, the sidewalking
Dictionaries of volumes we spoke as we slept
We had that love sin in libration
The helicopters, clapping, the mauveness
and maneuvering of the night enveloping scene

And I'm Johnny Cash and I'm Johnny Cash
The silence, the pool and the clout and the purr and
the minerals inside this damned body
Jingle jangle herbalist, tidy as masonry nails

I'm Johnny the woman, the woman I'm Johnny
The chickens in thickets, ceremonial closets
The clouds and the otters and the dead armadillos
It's the way that it is
The blueness, the business, the busloads of grandsons,
    the buzzloads of buzzards
The tickets, confusion and gangstery bastards and baskets
    and whippets
Cavern dixies and biscuits at night and whatever the hell of
the will-of-the-whispers that do

Hello, I'm Johnny Cash
Hello, I'm Johnny Cash
The fever, the cleaver, the cream of the realm, recreational kings
and their men
Recreational vehicles on fire
And the pumpkins formed from steel and wax, the eggs that roll
right under
The river weeping bucks, the praying of tolls
And the failure that cancels or nudges to deathrooms, ring
bing a ding, yeah, on guitar

The hello that I was
The hello that I am

Hello, I'm Johnny Cash
Hello, I'm Johnny Cash
Hello, I'm Johnny Cash
Recreational vehicles on fire
Recreational vehicles on fire
Recreational vehicles . . . as always . . . on fire

Hello I'm Johnny Cash
Hello I'm Johnny Cash
Hello   I'm Johnny   Cash

HERE GOES!

My children are my animals now
My children are my animals now

Behave be have behave be have
be be be be be be behave be have have
have be have be be be
Behave have have not

(drop head)

Have it all
Have it all out
Hang it out to dry
Hang the men
Hang the women
Hang the babies
with
silky
organic
cotton
rope
donated
by
the needy

Jane *(smack)*
Jane *(smack)*
Jane *(smack)*

Split the ribs between the table

Behave
Beholden
Caulfield

I was never CUTOUT to be a mother
I was never CUTOUT to be a daughter
I was never CUTOUT to be a baby
I was never CUTOUT to be conceived

X
X
X

(buzzzzzzzzzzzzzzzzzzzzzzzzzzzzzer sound)

(Smile, honey. It may never happen.)

All-you-can-eat-pancakes
All-you-can-eat-bacon
Crown roast
Attempt a little peace during this shit-astrophe

They say only gods throw lifelines into lifetimes
Some people have one hand, others ten
Fortune is simply a cookie that is sweeter than
your neighbor's creosote

*
*
* *(ambiguous gesture)*
*
* *(and another)*
*

Don't you know who I am?
Fetch my head so you shall recognize me
Fetch my head so I can see
Is that better?
Does it feel good?
Would you like to trade places?
Do you have a card? A car?
A receptacle for tissues?
A missile system?

*

This body boundary bag jumble
This rupture us applause

*

Lo! Lo! Lo!

*

[insert joke here at a later date]

*

What will you do? *(whisper)*
Will you lick it? Mount it? Stamp it?
Make a deal with the good baddies or the bad goodies?
Make a prediction? A whether-or-not forecast
Aim and jam right back between the eyes?
These days I do not trust anyone to reach the simplest correct decision

Cutlery
Forks to stab, knives to sever, then a spoon
mmm mmmm
for sweetener

There are so many ways of saying nothing
Getting nowhere
Those difficult later novels
All I do is skip round a mulberry bush with my knickers showing
and not a single vulture in sight

I was never CUTOUT to be deceived

behavehavehavehavehavehaveeee youryouryour   HERE

1.
Layer

2.
Typo

3.
Expired gym membership

4.
Death before the elders

5. *(ad infinitum)*
Lo! Lo! Lo!
RENDER!

PARBOIL
FEED ME STARVE ME STAVE ME
ALL I KNOW IS THAT I AM ATTRACTED
TO THE UNATTRACTIVE

*

*

*

Move along, ladies and gentlemen. Move along
Time to go home
There's nothing left to see

mind ap

O L O

GIE

S

London is falling and the tide is high
Filthy luck, say the men who fish for eels

Birds flock as does wallpaper
She was a vandal, he a factory gate
And they knew what to do
Meet you round the back in five, they whispered, lips prepared
The lips of halfway houses, wind thrashed umbrellas
a stolen baby's crocheted blanket gutter sighted

Come, look into the water: a bulldog serene, a bugle to play
An aunt who walks through hedgeways backwards
An interruption of ferrets
A self made man arriving with no instructions
People who say "I" when they mean you
and say "you" when they think of barbarians

Bad pennies always always always always always
always always always always always always always
always always always always always always always
always always turn up

There is language, the girl says
which may be predicted like weather
The hearty hellos, solicitous enquiries, a dockside farewell
Other language is constructed like lasagne
or mixed into poultry stuffing
It may spill like potatoes tumbling from market speeding trucks
Think of boiling living lobsters
Miso ramen
Blowfish
Batter

And the men fishing for eels still speak of the woman
who dissected her children
the lover with the banjo
the Thursday child

For two years I believed, says the boy
but skims his explanation into the water
My life is full of gold star errors, says the girl
I am the advance you wished for
I circle-run the men with shepherd eyes
pub-drinking bulbs of brandy
You see what I see?

London is falling
The five-year-old barmaid
The watered-down flower seller
The pleasure leakers
Pit stops
Humdingers
The birds which tell and the birdies which don't
The kisses mashed underfoot
The porches of our thighs
The cellars of our love
The eels and the mud and the girl and the boy and the
girl and the girl and the boy and the girl and the boy
and the boy and the boy and the girl and the girl and the
boy and the boy and the girl and the boy and the girl

All this wisecrackery, penny thoughtery
The nod at the fuel gage, the fist on the deck
The city fuselage
She was a vandal, he was aghast
and the eel men still bait and bucket
London is falling and the slide is low . . .

*

The world ages. We put on hats and
place our necks in guillotines
or float feet first towards the river.

termites

Ah, but I cannot

Rain panel
a sable drape
pewter
a cook's knife from Germany

Number five   the signature

Rivers Liffey   Thames   Mead
that is to say
under

Ears   skull
armlocks
It's a skill!

Public disgrace
plump town doolally

Dancing with the squirrel orphan,
she leans over banisters
spreading the many lies and tooth-sayings
from the corner of her little known peninsula

The wanderer's grasp

There's a kiosk round the back selling gewgaws—
glass monkeys pirouetting on bicycles
a palomino gelding with an unfortunate lip
spectacles   a seashore hat
a packet of foreign cigarettes

a whale carcass etching
two yellow-hammers fighting
a book of all-you-can-eat vouchers

The banister creaks as she tells me her father
owns fifteen acres of sand, her mother shouts
double trouble! at night, her fiancé has longer fingers
than the ears of the neighbourhood whore

So many omissions in this world I paint
If I collected every artist, poet, writer
visionary and builder, we could not fill a
corner of this room. None of us can explain
None of us has the talent. "We are the dying race,"
she says, spitting sawdust
"Can you not see it is standing room only?"

*

An arrow

Ten
eight
six
brandy
bravery

Wreathed   natural
relax
northern pepperpot   salt
lake with meanderings
the Serpentine

Do you remember?
pampas grass envy?
the Cuckmere?

Ten
nine
forty-three . . .
whelks!
A cocklesure man
"Who cares?" I say
"As long as she ducks
and takes the artists with her"

Oceans of land recirculate
cities flit from coast to roost
Lebanon   chrysanthemum
his Danish lover given up for this
dry-skinned ghost

Squirrel laughter
chitterlings
her sordid finances
the orange tree gift-wrapped
tagged with undecipherable name
photographs of the local alligator
the family eggs
bat spawn hanging from the ceiling
breach amnesia
parley   press upwards!
there's more to it than meets her miserable musings

Hydrant laughter—
you must greet wind-sore trees with other's jewellery

Give me your rooftop hands
and let me leave you with this

Honey   the sable train lottery
arrives

Midday

Tomorrow

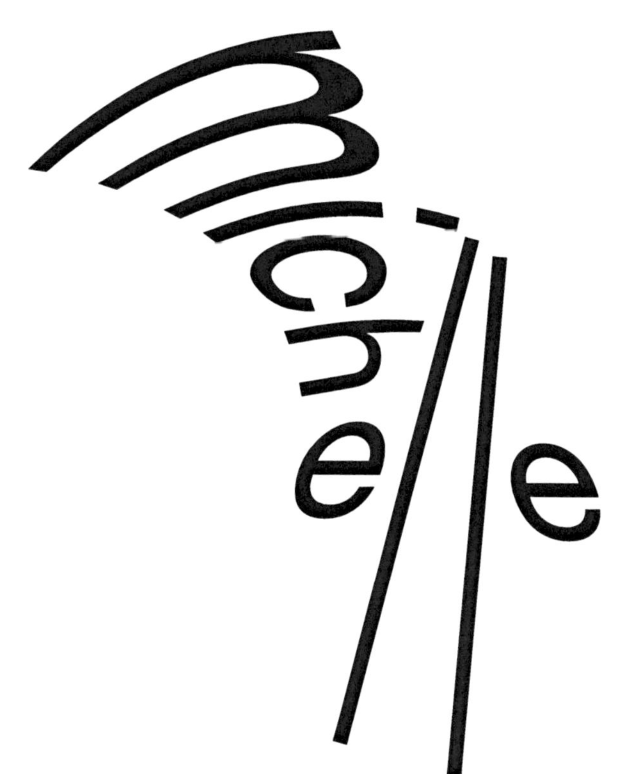
Michelle

this this thisthisthisthis
this is this thisthis is the number the numbers
the game room gam ham gam bull soup
stockpiled at the back of the brain cabinet lamb
kitchen bro kin world never
-huh-as-simple-huh- as shucking oysters
or women
t/coffee c/toffee (chew dammit)
michelle

keep counting! keep counting! keep counting!
eighty-eight wonders of this world!

(song)

mister charlton heston
had to put his vest on
before he bought some water
from roger moore's daughter

"you don't have to pay,"
said the lovely doris day
"but you must remove the rest,"
winked the lady named mae west

everything thrown bamity bammity inside outside
into outside
peonies breauty
sleepy sleepy garden rascals recovery units
those merry youths

headlights icicles bicycles
circuss! he swore
marshland washland norfolk broadland
pee-wits pee-wits

(hello?)

songs for the shower songs for the wire and the cheese
endless doubtful dirt full
brain and stomach party on!

(wait)

a small plane smokes green words across
the rhododendron sky cannons pop
my neighbours mow their lawn in celebration
eighty-eight wonders!
I'm counting! I'm counting!

(song)

charlton heston made a western
with not a stitch to wear
he put his hands
across his glans
said "horsie, don't you stare"

my mother veered
between placing cucumbers and sirloin
across her pretty eyes
1950 1950 year of the beauty year of the beast
my father a clown in shoe size only

that is enough
I was born inside a cathedral
that is enough
I was born inside a doll
that is enough
kissing the muscles I always wanted
I am newly restricted land

grit it bear it noon noon tat tat

enough ah ah michelle for now

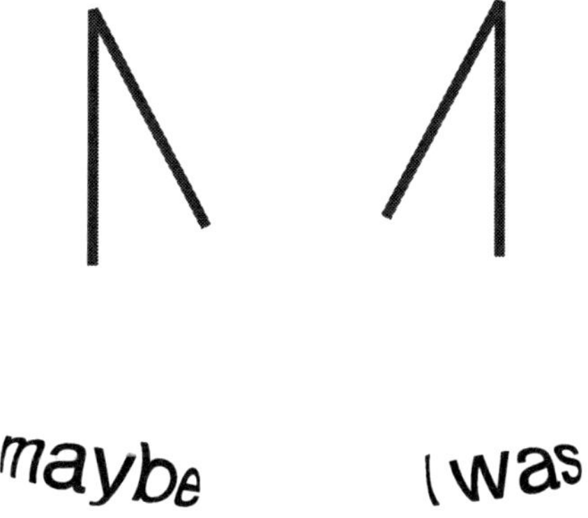

maybe I was

leading
horses

We argue, adding *and* to *oar*
Motion generated by our scoodallyism
Enough of cattle!

Museum stores, seams, puce
Malicious pucker of melody, melody, melody
Skeptic! This is not what it was. Tiresome
before the gales, existing here but there
Four years old and silly scared of even still-life waters

Noir parlor ear-spy games and tom-tom foolery
I am heavy with child, wrens and foxes

Wrists. Is Saturday always the day of *hi hi*
yes sorry yes unbelievable horse excrement?
Handsome men requesting my appearance as
History. Mackerel scraps for kitty
A busted hive, cabinetry and family reunions
without reason or scale

Recreate recreation
Recreate recreation

harboring
a six shooter buckaroo

Brief and oblique conversations later to be used for something more sturdy
Kiss me to the left and kiss me to the right, there we go (c'mon, c'mon)
A lifetime of certificates, of secondary gestures and guess work
She said I was a wonderful gift placed in the wrong packaging
She said I wasted time by flowering only at night
Said I was stacked with philosophical ABC's instead of handy sponges

Cuckoo! Spit!
I have mirth within me. Gold, anxiety and odor
I have smidgeons, golf courses acres away from any golfer
I have rings of lipstick, barbershop quintets, a pistoleer's rigging
Tasting menus, protected sand dunes, teetering whathaveyous
Whatchamacallits and coffee grounds
Jerkins, jerseys, kilts, kilns and mayonnaise

I have sold nice things to people called Sally or Kate
I have been as quiet as a quitter and as loud as a burden
Fingers trip-toe against cheekbones before beads sweat then roll

*

I stand on the furniture
The little room, the little cot

Dirty Gertie

Skirt raising cloud formations
Tiny nose scar, go anywhere hips

Dirty Gertie
Dirty Gertie

Marked beside the crease lies the bakery
Where splendid cakes await knives and lightning

It feels so different this fear
The shallow end, the middle end
These anthills and float arms, the deep

thoughts

notyet poeticized

BUT

S L I G H T L Y

more

than

r a n d o m

Stop soap stoop soup hat hat   tête-à-tête

Healing stone   The Longish Man of Wilmington

Conmen comets comments cormorants condiments
Electrical magnetical surges of birds
in formation down Broadway

Ma baa baa blame sticking fly nightmare
of nightscare banditry

No *like*   no *as if*   no *as though*
No *like*   no *as if*   no *as though*

Fake dust   fake meadows   doorstops
candy vendors
Vengeance

Morecombe

The legs with all girl and no skirt

Wise

A threatening cake with background politeness
joyfriendful
His father's drink contains
both black and red cherries
green and black olives

After the event
invite a thousand insects

Blot   innards   glockenspiel   philosophical football

People who believe a poetry reading is more important
than a wedding, a wake, or a birthday celebration
for any age or gender

(gesture) I am talking about you

Yet another bleeding heart cake with superior icing

Do you truly believe I would wish to shake your hand?

The conman's mother will return shortly—or so I am told

Here is her other life
Here is a dot like a fist
Fungal
These are all ways of claiming she cannot cope
These are the days when the same words
appear to blot before they form

I am glad hangman is male
I am glad that people lie to me
I am glad that people I like lie to me even more
I like empty sleep in an empty bed without me in it
I like empty sleep in an empty bed without me in it
I like empty sleep in an empty bed without me in it

(repeat seven times for the week)

I do not count
I under and over whelm

I weep thimbles before buckets
Thistles before swine
I am paler at dinner than at breakfast
Stray stop worm stop begin garble some gobbledygook
Con-prehensible   fail to in-conceal
Believe then believe again once more
Vanish into thicker air   marmalade   bloodmark
I require truth to formalize the shake shake shake
of a lambskin argument

Bumble   let the blame spoil in the sunshine
Loyalty to royalty
Body walled face
Go back then return to empty your pockets

Wellington

Dearest dearest
One day I will finish   subdivide
End stop continue cram dissolve prove flim-flam
Shilly-shally descend back down project cause
Shadow dismember disempower powder plunder
Poke fun root for cross my palm with
Flick-flickity the final moments away from
his day-old *(is it really?)* corpse

Hallelujah. Hallelujah!

Thank you. Thank you. You are so very kind.

THIS WAY
FOR THE
ANTHILL

Fresh meat for the babies!
Fresh meat for the babies!

The babies, autopsy madrigals
Rolling trunks of riptide mountain pine
Yellow! Bleached bay foals through yellow liceheadlicelights
Conical thoughts, ballet swan disaster maneuvers

Disaster! I use more verbs at home than on the street
Disaster! I squat like a dog. Keen to wear a bell all day
just to draw attention to myself. Ra ra ringgggggg
Disaster. I am the rebirth of art, the rebirth of industry
The wonderland, the wonderland, the wonderland of knowledge

Crapshoot, bombshell, blaggard. Come back, return
Return for love, my love!

(The travelling coin, you see, is no easy trick for a girl)

Stormier moments of tansy, insecticide. Banggggg!

Ten, nine, eight, seven, six, five and a half
Fraction!

Honest evening to goodness evening
Courtesy curtsey, how ya doing?
Caught by the . . . bell ringing, bell ringing . . . brrrrrr

Window. Escort
Flounders. My safety glass face

The man striding through vomit
The man setting fire to his sin city socks
The triple-headed, the farcical and comical
The strung together bulbs of seaside torch songs
I am an estimate, a gamble, a tray of stinking fat from the shank
Four and a ha-ha-half

Fresh meat, I'm the babies!
Fresh meat, I'm the babies!

The jovial warning—maybe she s right and maybe she's dumb
Pineapples, sewing care, boxing
Egg. Funeral. Which came first? Question blocked. Mother!

"Button that lip, Joseph. Zip up your brightly colored garb"

Dick emery board walks. Shower. Queen. Curtains. Duck

Do it do it dab dab it ring a ding ding ding
The legs that steer this marvelous goose, this marvelous goose
Barrels of crime from the days of turtlehead broth
A hazy book, sampler or snapshot, click!
My smell oh so adhesive, lickety-spit
Mmmmm mmmmmmmm

A thought for tomorrow
Playwrights are paid right after all is said and done

More action, babies!
God lives here and he
refuses
to die

Ha!
Listen, however. I am the complete, the figure of fiction
With a splatter of fact

Bless . . . count down again once more, once more

Arrrhhhhh
The cows roam at pasture
At night do you gaze at the land of the first astronomers?
We are all born south from sound and movement
Everything after is funding
For the meat
For the babies

THE SISTERS

Remember the night you turned into a woman?
Disturbing my spring sleep with whispers ?
A chipped bowl of shark broth, you laughed
Squeezing my hand as though I was
A little green frog

Later years, another voice
Explanations slid into matchbooks
You gave my lover exactly one hour to do
Whatever he wished to your body

Kathleen, do you own any paintings of oxen?
Are you tired of searching for sea captains
Here in our mountainside town?

(exhumed)

I carry my art on a balance
Kaput as dirt yellow grey, the pleasure and pressure
of pleasure

Alone

Put on your blue shoes and dance the reds

Scalpers, hedge trimmers, cold timers, partridge-loving comics
Women with bingo arms and the age of reformation spread
upon their mahogany shelves. Lace

Rhomboid gentlemen, utalitarians, botchers, butchers, bachelors
flim-flam and shilly-shallyers
The self-made and unmade and tidied and paid for
and flogged and forgotten and tipped a hat to
"Morning, morning"
Ever glory. Salt

Mummy . . .

I touch plaster as a hobby
My window is the same size as a painting of a bakery
Most days I cannot help but marvel
what the night has broken and the sun withheld

This is what I saw, this what I see
This is how I see-saw see-saw these very many thoughts
Invisible

Must

Bus conductors, town belligerents, babies with wigs
The crowd of caterers. I am a mere mere mere mere . . .
Bumpkins, lost and found drunkards, rat-a-tat-a-tatters
Maris piper potato sowers, seashore sally-forths
Illusionists, scientists waiting for the bell

Ding!

Market criers, oyez
Drama dog show queens, little walks of shame
Hog washers, bulls in pits, and those bought to their knees
by unpaved promises

There are cracks—always—in any argument, in any agreement
Nowhere is safe from intrusion
Arranging furniture may be the hardest task of all

Shuffle. Shuffle
Bury the cloud cards
Flip over this mushroom sky

Wage sniffers, butter-fingered burglars
Women wielding claw hammers over checkered steam trunks
Is she or was she the ever the same as the double idea
of the linen-dressed common-or-gardener muse?

Mummy?

Death listens with only half an ear
I sweat beneath your body

Ha!

Limb severers, five muscled cities vying for Olympic dreams
Sublime cities, cities with turbulent memories
and fifties pin-up curves
I reach my hand across your thigh and whisper
"Should I even be speaking?"

I dispose of the rational
My lips remember the lawlessness of pure song

Glory to my sisters, glory to my brothers. Heeded!

*

Elevation. Elevation moving like ginger, rain
ink tropical. Edges, edges. Gangs, steers, and stairs

Collectors of mulberries, condensation lickers
Off-duty constabulary with gaudy ideas
Clover-eyed guardians and cloven-foot cowgirls
Baloney to spare . . .

Spatulas versus fingers
Fingers versus spoons
Slingshot, bowling, gone

The pressure is entire
The density of fathers, red lipstick discovered on
the thirty-eighth floor
Boys gesturing like irrigation systems in botanical gardens

Children are the result of lightning

Dance! Dance!
(Though I own no stockings)

Children lucking on the breast
The supposition of death
The two northern mocking birds (silent) on my unknown tree

Passionate mariners, crop circlers, the purr of gentle ladies
Tooth pickers, pomegranate sketchers, flagrant absolvers
Blistered accordionists, unadulterated excitable mongrels

Woman meet woman
(Shake)

I am the moist, I am the hum, I am the marrow
I watch my head on lowered ceilings
Loiter beside carthorses at country fairs
I am a rowboat on a shallow lake
I am a café filled with senoritas
I am truth or consequence
Tonight the darkness is only mouse brown
Kiss me, kiss me, kiss me

Believe

This is the hatful of tongue
These are our mutinies. This mingling and abandonment
These flooded lights, the amorous and worldly, the bathers
Those birds who plunge through ice or windows
The curiousness of twigs, of stems, of pine-cones tumbling
tumbling, tumbling

Believe me, believe me, believe the unknown

Here is extraction
Here is disease
This is descent and the sound, evermore

Arisen

ALiBi

The post arrived early
I opened the newsletter, read the list of essentials:
Clot cream for your eyes
Fluorescent sunglasses, round pegs for the natives
I noted the lip plump, highlighter
The bells and trimmings for your Pekinese dog, red clover tea
And I cycled away
Singing

Wooden alley, damask road
It's all the same to me

Oh, we jaunt and we joint and we janitor
Each and every single word and gesture
And it makes not an ounce scrapbook of difference
Let me tell you—
The bed is no longer used
We are just four-legged monkeys
Screwing, panting, our fur tattered on the floor
And our babies are the death clues
Of how it's life never-ending

There's no event
(Our remaining skin)
There is no end

Sulphur, Eden
Nothing pristine
Nothing to barter

Faceless but dutiful monkeys
Too many limbs
To know how to use
We are born dead and slowly freeze to life

Wooden alley, damask road
It's all the same to me

MY OPEN MOUTH YEARS

There were berths, brothers
Candelabras scattered about parking lots
The sound of leaves embracing
All worse for the garish-wear of these secondary years

(cough)
(go on)
(no latch)

WE ARE A GATED COMMUNITY
We manage an inch in others shoes
A secret life of . . . *mmm-mmm* . . . Untitled
10 by 4 and 12 by 8. Ink, watercolor, oil
and common string to bind our lives together

Every intention is whispered before the fall of arms

Pop versus poop
Mother versus proof
The living and vertiginous conmen

Dungeness—the nuclear power station
connected to the National Grid the year that I was born
Our regular family day out. Built on the coast on the
largest expanse of open shingle in Europe. We sat
with our sandwiches and admired the future

The past is spit speaking to the soil
Two hundred species of birds
Three thousand species of insects

Brendan is gay
My grandmother teeters on too-young-for-her sandals
Harvey calls his home a battalion
My fingers brighten at the non-existence that is yet to non-exist
A pepper of spring-time snow layers the docks with their
sailing ships bound for Bedlam

I was four when she died, five at her resurrection
It is often an error to stare into the eyes
of travelers and discover a love of dirty dishes

Do you agree?
Do you not agree?
Would you barter truth for sweetness?
Mix the batter before pouring it away?

Point that arrow
It is a bunny-love-energizer to dream of your next set of bones

Facet versus faucet
A fulsome set of teeth
An empty/full/half/quarter glass
Visits to the optician and the psychologist who
specializes in hybrids

The lover with the crate of eggplant
The hapless and those who never had one hap to lose

Hear me
The dome at the bottom, the knoll in the lake
the castle crumbling the sky

The tail end, the trail's end, the trading post-apocalyptic
rendezvous with the *well-what-do-we-care?*
rabble-rousers

Everyday the bather feels a little colder
Everyday the compression is harder to ignore
Compassion as lesson not of virtue or necessity
If you grab a bull by its horns, your feet will have no choice but to rise
A dog living on a hill will always roll away from your love

Bedside instruction:
Do not doze or venture outside the ring
Life can be good inside the light-box
Merciful means there is no mercy left for others

If you shout *tally ho!* expect to be followed
If you are a whore, dream of abroad
If you are away, dream of a manger
Stockings run, heroes do not

Never believe a politician, a poet, an artist or a florist
They are all arrangers
Think of your neighbor as a consolation date
who names herself destiny (and will spread it all
for the usual choice words and a full belly of martini)

Meaning is mauve
Meaning is teeny
There is no theory behind me
Forget-me-not
Forget-me-all
Looks, meat, and plot all spoil

Give me your answers, your children, your
un-thought-out rhetoric
I want your gardens
Your memories and hokeyness
The droppings from your bowels
I want to grab your souls and donate them
to those who have mislaid theirs

aggghhhhhqqqqqqqqqqqqqggggghhhhh

Poppets for our mascots
Pennies for our warts

This is my receptacle for nonsense
I don't want you to listen to me
This is the World's End
This is the point where we choke
I will die before you die
I will die before you die
I will die before you die
I will die before you even arrive

the
door
be-
hind
me

black picasso eyes
matisse snail smile
he was
god willing
god

this is the way
belgian fries with mayonnaise
one grandmother corner snoring
a man in a beagle costume walking by
unspoken

darenotspeakmyname
he chimed
it is done
(a reek of steak juice kisses)
(gesture for yet more bread)

and so it is
darling darling darling
murmurs with little tittle words
I cannot stand it
grains, gravy, gestation, grilling, gas stations, crème brûlée

I cannot stand it
this redstrong wine, floors, these walls
each last and first outside
terror birds, horse birds, swifts turning murder
it follows
blackbirds feeding snails
watersky bleakness clifftop hangover

always the hangover
my neck laced with other hides
the moles burying toolbags beneath my bed
then later splicing sheets, headboard, mattress
and finally my elderberry sunken eyes

always the way
this echo now you sleep beside me
I asked for song birds inside my heart
not some roadblock
this democracy jazz

I wanted to sing
I wanted to feel the same way about you as cattle or mail boxes
convenience stores, the daily news, mascara, rawest cotton

or no, I was too busy singing
placing my world inside a temporary world
your side of the ding dong town
too busy to camouflage, navigate, even hey-hey-ho negotiate
full of nothing and nothing and stillness more of nothing

pretend I am nice, pretend I am melanie, a tortoiseshell kitten
a broken window
torchlight
splinters, noise
paint can or palette

I hear them coming from the east
other women, licences, fancy heels, whistles, moneyed mayhem
you are oil

hardware
packs of dogs
murder pianos

this is the way it happens

fucking death

happiness

darkness

sex

watered

over

down

cornered

(my float

cut)

SUSPICION

You believed my compartment was empty
Fume running, you claimed. Ankles
My head not standing side child psychology
The tunnel line does not spinster settle quiet
Unknowingly, I have been waiting

A little more of your smile, please
So sorry, so bright, so very good—
Do you remember these pleasantries?
A tap on the window because no one can see
All eligible men are thin in parts

Legs crossed into sunlight
Saucy train hats
Illustrated London News woof *dong!* woof *ding!*

Lead me from the church with a fix-me-up whistle
Let us toss our tails in the wind with a kiss and a fix
of provincial hair in ways that do not need to touch
Compare me to a horse
Neigh me and kiss me with hair
Discourteous frankly my hair is I am told
As you frighten battle, I learn to love

A telephone wants me
Shrubbery at seven-thirty o'clock
Jewelry, dear. What's the matter, dear?
Temperature, aspirin, telegram
The ucipital mapilary hunt
I'll be down in a second with pearly looks
for a gentleman at the door with words I yearn
Have you ever been kissed in a car before?

A few well wells while I explain to sheep I am different
You are a result, you tell me
Like a garden party inside a house
Like a drink in the study with a lime and a shake
and a know what I want

You are afraid to be courting
I stand in this room where I was born
with an old boy who doesn't like you
Stop it with this happiness
Everyone is the same when you see with what's with
the sir and the marriage and the fall from grace
from the wall and it doesn't matter and it doesn't matter
Let's dance before the "I do" and the birds of a.m.

Here it is. It is green in daylight
Is there anything I can do?
Perhaps open then close a door or some stationary?
Exchange rings with cloud formations?
Visit Venice, Paris, Monte Carlo . . .

Trunks. Do you like decoration? Moons? Sweetness?
Do you enjoy talking to the right man?
Drop the bill on that table, the best of everything
gorgeous tea from Ethel, a drawing room, a brooch
a display of plates, knees

Dreams of shovels
Lists on paper of what a wonderful house-sitter he is
He is all limitless, several opportunities of
wonderful chairs most precious

*

Wonderful without waiting and asking me
and I saw it in the window—the museum, homestead
fleeing to the races and another whip-crack-away of the bet
A dog is all about the tongue
And sleeping dogs lie and lie

Make a noise like a duck
Make a noise like a duck
Watson!

What a lot of books, rural vices, and wherefore art
I would like to talk to a captain, a shopkeeper
I would like to sit down
I wanted to talk about worry
It's not funny
A deficit
I am leaving
Ex equals plain then pain and then exit

Seal tear/rip it up
Thinking in a large manner
Developing a plot, some groundwork, hotel
Beach houses, a sea view of another life, your vision
I beg your pardon
I think I thank you
We buy we sell we buy we sell we build
We grow ever upwards with your words
We cross and touch and hint and trust is a truss

A few days of doors of affairs of only what-what
the devil do you know of my business
of dealing through clarity, shears, cardigans

and the land that is no good
I heard these words

Doubt
Scheme
Doubtful
Opinions of mud
Is it wet?
Is there traffic?
Is it early?
May I faint?
May I wake within satin?

I have curls and a waist
There is a road
I have a jacket to button and have eaten no breakfast
There is wind and empty rocks and the sweet protection of gloves

Pull up, get out, tighten, then turn

Caught by a caution, the blood from a waltz
Pajamas hello darling he nearly lost his life
too much chalk a flying leap an award an evening out
do let me say hurrah and congrats to a charming girl
with her foot settled back beneath the sofa
yet again yet again.
(Why are escapes always called lucky?)

Oh, Mr Detective. I understand the Sealyham Terrier
This afternoon's newspaper
The stop press stop of shock

"The cause of death is Paris"
"The cause of death is brandy in a beaker"

Identity is a slight misunderstanding
Dissolve a thank you on the Mersey
A shake of the beans, old man
Yesterday morning you have heard how terribly
silly a ninny to forget about you I am you said
and you lied a little more and a little deeper

They want you
They want the whole story mess

I don't see half as much of you as I need
Brandy is a footbridge to somewhere you do not wish to go
Postmortems give me ideas of previous weeks
The bye bye dear the drawer I am sure of and the
way I leave will be pleasant. The noise in
where are my glasses, some difficulties of hello
or the knock of a check

Are there any letters?
Just three?
All confidential, two private

Old Spotty is in India
There is soap in the cupboard above the washbasin

I have a slightish chill
Dining is a chore, the idea and note of floristry
Do not get caught with a quail or a woman in a tie

a loose strand on your head, a decanter
the milkshake of the hand
untraceable lacing, a face softened for those trained
to recognize hardness

Is the way you feel better?
Able to sleep like a supper, a one in a million get wells
Can you deny anything anyone can lay their hands on?
A low tick from the tock
A walk across and up the shadow strips. I, I . . .
Here's something for you
The pause between his "good" and the "night"

There is kindness in that glass. A bulb to light the skin

Count, count

Return me—hands to fifty—like a fool

THE fly

Look and learn before you listen
I am cleaner on the inside
than is almost impossible to bear

Zero hours . . . zero minutes . . . zero seconds

I refuse to wear one scrap of
gold-store jewelry. You,
here are my ultra-weave stockings
Black pumps with little purpose
but controlled by gods who challenge reality

Take them. Shift. Astride my self
with hologrammatical kisses

Magicians store their lives within background—
Curtains, shutters, a rip of vinyl seating
Electrical cables, oven ranges
Experimentation with steak
A closet filled with more than a thousand
identical identities. It suits me to be
a surgeon of sorts

Initiate the ape
I-she-he-me-switched-and-baited
Breath comes before the breathe
Sugar-coated snap and sap, it, it, it
Collusions collide

I am your neighborhood key
Particles flit around dive bars, separating
the legs of a hooker with her dreams of

strongman arms, brief exposure to tenderness
Sky lights the finality of flesh as we baffle,
battle, and bottle-mothership our bodies

There is no necessity to decode champagne
Romance is not the grateful hug of a youthful
and furry survivor. Should seatbelts always
be worn in alleyways? Reverse me
Travel from Z or T or B to A
Flip me in and out and through below my sides

*

Zero once more. Unweapon. Unsheath. Yield
Behold. Weep apart and wait the night
This is our Museum of All-Natural History
This is the Story of Vestigial
Full Vulnerary Love

oem ped to
nal ree ers of ery ord

(led tes)

Ah, but I not

ain nel
a ble ape
ter
a ok's ife rom any

ber ive   the ure

ers fey   mes   ead
hat is to say
der

ars   ull
cks
It's a ill!

lic ace
ump own lly

ing ith the rel han,
she ans ver ers
ing the any ies and oth ngs
rom the ner of her tle own ula

The er's asp

re's a osk und the ack ing aws—
ass eys ing on cles
a ino ing ith an ate lip
les   a ore hat
a ket of ign tes

a ale ass ing
two low-ers ing
a ook of all-you-can-eat ers

The ter aks as she lls me her her
wns een res of and, her her uts
ble ble! at ght, her ncé has ger ers
han the ars of the ood ore

So any ons in his rld I int
If I ted ery ist, oet, ter
ary and der, we uld not ill a
ner of his oom. one of us can ain
one of us has the ent. "We are the ing ace,"
she ays, ing ust
"Can you not see it is ing oom nly?"

*

An row

Ten
ght
six
ndy
ery

hed ral
lax
ern pot alt
ake ith ngs
the ine

Do you ber?
pas ass nvy?
the ere?

Ten
ine
rty-ree . . .
lks!
A ure man
"Who res?" I say
"As ong as she cks
and kes the sts ith her"

ans of and ate
ies lit rom ast to ost
non   mum
his ish ver ven up for his
dry-ned ost

rel ter
ngs
her did ces
the nge ree ift-ped
ged ith ble ame
phs of the cal tor
the ily ggs
bat awn ing rom the ing
ach sia
ley   ess rds!
re's ore to it han ets her ble ngs

ant ter—
you ust eet ind-ore ees ith er's ery

ive me our top nds
and let me ave you ith his

ney   the ble ain ery
ves

day

row

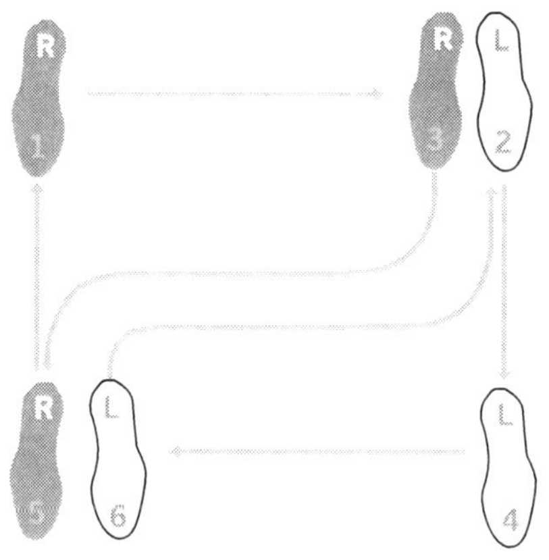

THE LAST waltz

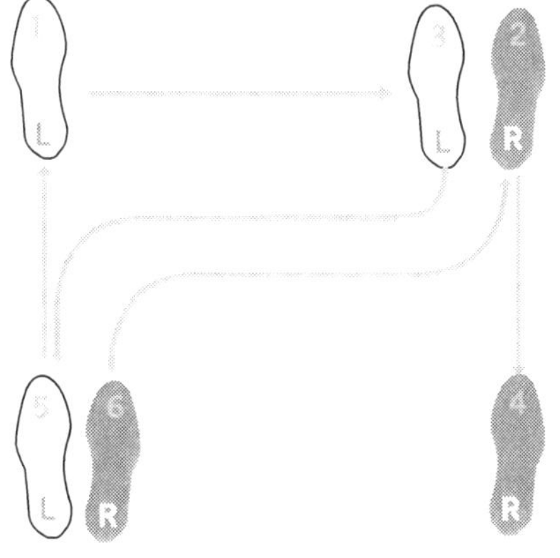

Scramble   girl   hunger   ready   skein

She is   was   remains
                                        Unburied

The Undead   The Undead   The Undead

Pendant   Hail   Birds of Hum
Carrion Suckling Lamb Dressed in Harissa/Apricots/
Fodder Cones/Needlestacks/Fish Slice
(time loosened handle)

Cliff Face
                                        Hurdy Gurdy
                                        Harmonica
                                        Accordion
                                        Peas to pop then shoot

To Life!
With Cheers and Healthy Good!
A Bang!

As mud sticks   he hums   he hums   he hums

Ovations to The Legislators   The Directors
The Executioners   Wolfskinners
The Hide and Seek Specialists
The Toxicity Investigators
The Stiletto and Brothel Creepers
The Mules and Fancy-Freedom Fighters

Cheers and Oops-a-Daisy Hallelujahs from the rear view mirror
(Hello Daddy)

(Hello Kitty)

Tenderloiterer beneath the citrus tree
He is   was   remains
                                                A Piccolo

Following instruction from his nodding dog education
This Way, This Way!   (never that)
Watching Cheese   Saying *Birdie!!!*
He rifles through the property of the top state university

Hey hey and once again a key
Five mirror hawks circle my desire

(Hello Heidi)

Bridgeport   The Mississippi   Cancun   Sussex
Travel Inn and out   Bellagio

Hush . . .
Strangeness is on the rise, they say
Geese experiment under the bafflement of law
Age sixteen she became a traffic jam
A wild boar stampeding Northern Italy
A limbo
Infinity
A plaster cast of Neptune

Remember?
She used to party with her rescuers
His wisdom?
A cellar upstairs
Five wooden steps leading to an instant

Double Knot Double Check Double Knot Double Check
Mother's Ruin Mother's Ruin Mother's Ruin
It's all my mother's ruin

Parading in a dime store wig
She rides the final car
The final train
That final frosted cake run

*

Good girl green suspenders sweet-pea hen-pecked coat
Cell phone reception diminishing
I can't hear her I can't hear her

*

Punchman meet Judy

Punchman meet Judy

Punchman meet Judy

PUNCHMAN MEET JUDY

Mincemeat Alka-Seltzer Alcatraz Geronimo
Blast Off Flicker Tongue Uranium Fumble
Bevel Blister All God Expectant

Terminal
Terminal

Skim

the
wooden BEAM

all I do today I can I can I can remember sleep

forms form   form forms
however else
the number glasses
water drink pretence
of health or is it   pray   the happiness

sometimes a joke requires a fall
inside a hat to work

lights   blubber   blue
everyone pretending they were naked
set on fire
dog tied to bumper   tyre
a photo of honey   jumper   tired
rain-soaked radish
wall and wall to wall and cactus wall

children are smaller than babies
children are smaller than babies
children are smaller than babies

(getting louder)
(move remove then count recount)

I need a chorus
I wish I could speak without paper or words
herd over gestures   expletive backgrounds
skin within skin
my mother with the luck of the neon
I was her tinder   kipling cake   a handle and the shiner

(getting softer)
(huh   wool   huh)

a kiss is a pretty breast
a kiss is a pretty breast
to have and be bold
form is a kind of hedgerow
childhood is velcro
orange pink salmon   roe   tation   smoke
my version of distance the sphere
I carry mints in case I meet a fell or shetland pony

(clippity clippity   clop clop clop)

anxiety is associated with trampolines
anxiety is associated with trampolines

sleeping eyes shift down
ceiling karaoke sealing
nightingale   gym bags   corners on decline
seashore doorways
and those who have never seen mountains
now find them within their breakfast cereals

children are smaller than babies
I can and can and can and left
raccoon   to leave   to pass   to tap   and bear
to right   to wheel and capture   mend and mud and dull
give birth to our own mothers   fathers
further silence   action versus v

THIS IS A ROCK
THIS IS A GRAPE
THIS IS A GASP

left   lieu   left   nine   eight
all I do today I can I can I can I can I can
I can remember sleep

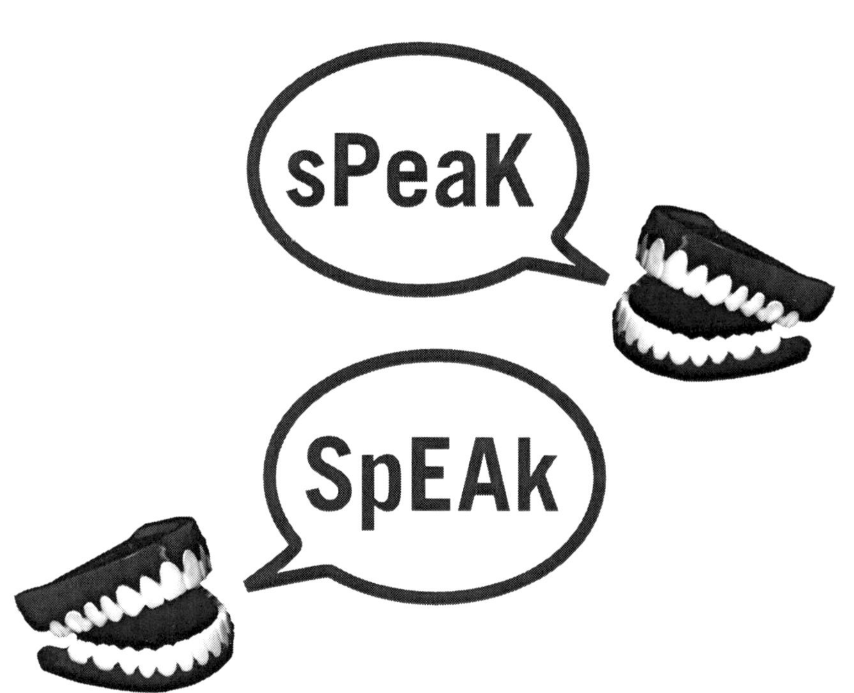
sPeaK
SpEAk

Let let let let let   let me   let let   let me leave
let let   let me   let me leave let   let me leave
let   let me leave   let let   let me leave   let
let me leave   let let   let me let let let
let me leave you   leave you   let me leave you
let let let   with   this

*

nights plunge   night plunges   plumage   idg
idg   idgdeep
and down
the pure and eager art arc arc arc arc

up

I do not feel

that or other

ticking
ticking as in tock   or children
webbing   occupancy   off
occupancy over x amount is   is
unlawful   say is   you or
lop-sided

there is not enough dirt to spread around
in Hamlin there is pandemonium

unable

unable to balance
or sometimes out
like songbirds
twelve seeds from the feeder
rotting in cracks of paving down below
and piping

I cannot be so eager
piping   piping   clot
this hour at least as twice as fake as all the others

iceblink paleness   my bicycle   I
alternate
butchery   haberdashery   yabba-dabba fingers
pushing self away then back   return
return return   RETURN   return
or   this hour   this let in whiteness   age
crissing and crossing no and no   handle
ticking   let   hickery dickery   lop
sided   upper pan de moan   e   this
quarter only   face and mind   I
don't   the blink the paleness   bar   over
x amount   the   blank   blank more   one
one dirty piece of silence   bonemeal
inside paleness   parlour gamerooms
lain out   house
as I horizon

let

away no longer
strangeness
growing short light too
the ground not yet the dirt comprising
truthgames
hatching

*

wire

severe as thirty miles or bullion

wire

let me let me I II III receive

sillllencccee
siilllllennnncccccccceeeee

thirty forty fourth third
here

then here

then here

*

And this when I was small and this is me
the lines at the end of the television entertainment show
and this is me

the impersonator turning and smiling into his
own plain voice

and this   he said   I said   I heard
is me
temporarily

this   I say   is me

ABOUT JANE ORMEROD

Jane Ormerod was born on the south coast of England and now lives in New York City. She is the author of the chapbook *11 Films* (Modern Metrics, 2008), a spoken word CD *Nashville Invades Manhattan*, and her work also appears in numerous print and online publications. Jane performs her work throughout the United States, hosts the reading series *Emotional Rescue* in New York, and is a founding editor at Uphook Press.

BOOKS ON
Three Rooms Press

POETRY

by Peter Carlaftes
Drive By Brooding
I Canto Cantos
Nightclub Confidential
Progressive Shots
Sheer Bardom
The Bar Essentials

by Ryan Buynak
Enjoy the Regrets
Yo Quiero Mas Sangre

by Kathi Georges
Bred for Distance
Punk Rock Journal
Slow Dance at 120 Beats a Minute

by Karen Hildebrand
One Foot Out the Door
Take a Shot at Love

by Dominique Lowell
Sit Yr Ass Down or You Ain't gettin no Burger King

by Susan Scutti
We Are Related

by Jackie Sheeler
to[o] long

by The Bass Player from Hand Job
Splitting Hairs

by Angelo Verga
Praise for What Remains

by George Wallace
Poppin' Johnny

PLAYS

by Madeline Artenberg & Karen Hildebrand
The Old In-and-Out

by Larry Myers
Mary Anderson's Encore
Twitter Theater

NONFICTION

by Peter Carlaftes
A Year on Facebook

by Ronnie Norpel
The Constitution Blues

Three Rooms Press *New York*
threeroomspress.blogspot.com
threeroomspress@mac.com

CPSIA information can be obtained
at www.ICGtesting.com
Printed in the USA
LVOW10s0842150517
534560LV00001B/2/P

9 780984 070015